FIFTY JUBILEE POEMS

Raphael (1483–1520)
Study for the Figure of Poetry, c.1510

FIFTY
JUBILEE
POEMS

The Queen's Golden Jubilee
Poetry Competition 2002

COVER ILLUSTRATIONS

The front cover shows the reverse of the Golden Jubilee
Poetry Medal which is based on Raphael's drawing *Study for the Figure
of Poetry* (see below). The back cover illustrates the obverse of the medal
showing the same image of The Queen's head as that used for the Golden
Jubilee Medal, which was based on a relief plaster model created by the
sculptor Ian Rank-Broadley. The medals are 54mm
in diameter and have been produced in gold, silver
and bronze versions.

FRONTISPIECE

This beautiful black chalk drawing was made in
preparation for Raphael's fresco of the personification of Poetry
on the vault of one of the Pope's apartments – the Stanza della Segnatura –
in the Vatican Palace, Rome. The room was decorated with allegories of
Theology, Philosophy and Jurisprudence, as well as Poetry – subjects that
were appropriate for the room's use as the library of Pope Julius II. The
winged Muse of Poetry holds a book and a lyre. The drawing has been part
of the Royal Collection since the reign of Charles II (1660–85)
and is kept in the Royal Library at
Windsor Castle.

Published by Royal Collection Enterprises Limited,
St James's Palace, London SW1A 1JR

ISBN 1 902163 20 6

British Library Cataloguing in Publication Data
A catalogue record for this book is available from the British Library.

Produced by Book Production Consultants PLC, Cambridge
Printed and bound in Great Britain by The Wolsey Press, Ipswich
Designed by Dalrymple

Contents

Introduction

POETRY HAS ALWAYS BEEN a distinct and distinctive part of our national life: the form we turn to – as individuals and collectively – at moments of celebration, crisis or intensity. It is something we do well, something we are proud of, and something that tells us important truths about ourselves.

As Poet Laureate, it seemed to me vital and inevitable that poetry should be a central part of Her Majesty The Queen's Golden Jubilee. It also seemed important that it should be included in a way that involved a large number of people, all raising their different voices, expressing their different identities.

The Golden Jubilee Poetry Competition was organised to make this happen. In October 2001 I wrote to every school in the country, asking them to encourage their pupils to write poems about some aspect of the last fifty years. The rules for the competition allowed each school to select up to three entries for each of three age bands (7 to 11, 11 to 14, and 14 to 18). All the entries were assessed by a team of readers provided by the National Association for the Teaching of English (NATE) and the Poetry Society. By early May 2002, these readers had chosen the best 125 poems from each section, which were passed to a panel of judges for a final decision. The judges were John Agard, Carol Ann Duffy, U. A. Fanthorpe, Michael Longley and myself.

We selected three entries from each of the three age categories to receive the specially commissioned gold, silver and bronze medals. The design of these medals, which were presented to the winners by The Queen at Buckingham Palace on 9 July 2002, is based on Raphael's *Study for the Figure of Poetry*, a chalk drawing which has been in the Royal Collection for over three hundred years. In addition to the poems by the nine medal winners, this book contains forty-one other poems we especially liked. It was our hope that the diversity as well as the energy of our poetic cultures would be evident in the long-listed poems. We were not disappointed and I believe that this selection of *Fifty Jubilee Poems* is a cause for celebration, as well as an act of celebration.

Every school participating in the competition will receive two free copies of this book.

I doubt whether there has ever been a larger poetry competition, which means that a large number of people have been involved in its organisation. I am very grateful to them all: to Her Majesty The Queen for authorising the competition, and presenting the medals to the winners; to the final panel of judges; to Sir Michael Peat, Sir John Parsons, Edward Hewlett, Ailsa Anderson and Morag Reavley at Buckingham Palace; to Tony Littlechild of Book Production Consultants, and to Robert Dalrymple; to Gary McKenzie, Paula Kitching and Amanda Woodham of the Department for Education and Skills; to Iain Finlayson of the Scottish Executive Education Department; to Keith Davies of the Welsh Assembly Government Department for Training and Education; to Valerie Steele of the Northern Ireland Department of Culture, Arts and Leisure; to Christina Patterson and Martin Colthorpe of the Poetry Society, whose advice and imaginative hard work were indispensable; to Kathryn Samson, who designed the competition booklet; and to Trevor Millum and his colleagues at NATE and the readers they suggested. A special debt of gratitude is also owed to John Sunley and his fellow trustees of the Bernard Sunley Charitable Foundation for funding the production of this book.

Finally, I would like to thank all those who entered the competition, and congratulate not only the three winners in each age category, but also those who wrote the other forty-one poems in this book. Their success celebrates poetry itself, as it also celebrates the Golden Jubilee.

ANDREW MOTION
Poet Laureate

Aberfan 21st October 1966

Tony Managh

'In that silence you couldn't hear a bird or a child'
Aberfan resident

In Aberfan it was so quiet,
You could hear the burning tears fall,
Hurting,
Heart-broken.

In Aberfan it was so quiet,
You could hear faces crumpling softly,
Loving,
Lonely.

In Aberfan it was so quiet,
You could hear hearts breaking,
No laughter,
No life.

In Aberfan it was so quiet,
You could hear empty arms aching,
Slipping,
Sliding.

In Aberfan it was so quiet,
You could hear The Queen hugging her own
Kids
Hard …

Tony Managh, aged 11, is a pupil at Park Junior School,
Wellington, Shropshire.

Inviting the Queen to Tea …

Louise Shaw

Dear Queen,
I hope you have a space suit,
For we are going to tea on Mars,
Please come,
Louise.
P.S. 5.30 sharp.

Dear Queen,
Please meet me at the space station, Florida,
For we are going on the 5.40 rocket,
Please come,
Louise.
P.S. Please come in that lovely pink dress for the rocket.

Dear Queen,
As you must recognise me, I will be wearing
   my blue frilly dress,
I'll be with four friends,
Please come,
Louise.
P.S. Oh, do come.

Dear Queen,
I hope you like roast beef, mashed potatoes and jelly
   with cream and strawberries,
Please come,
Louise.
R.S.V.P.

Dear Louise,
Yes, I love roast beef, mashed potatoes and mushy peas.
And yes, I have a space suit and I'd love to come.
Yours sincerely
   Elizabeth
P.S. *I will wear my pink dress.*

Louise Shaw, aged 8, is a pupil at St Martin's Church of
England Primary School, Dorking, Surrey.

The Jubilee Cat

Eden Latham

Pussy cat, pussy cat, where have you been?
I've been in London to visit the Queen.

Pussy cat, pussy cat, what did you see?
I saw the Queen getting ready for her Jubilee.

I bet you didn't see her sneeze!
I did.
I bet you didn't sit on her knees!
I did.

And she said, Pussy cat, pussy cat, what are you doing here?
Would you like a sip of my Jubilee beer?

I said, 'No, thank you, Queen, I'm not yet eighteen,
But I'd appreciate a tickle and some royal cream.'

So the Queen clicked her fingers and called 'Daphne, come here'
And in a twitch of my whiskers a maid did appear.

She said, Daphne, Daphne, milk the royal cow
I need a jug of cream for this pussy right now.

And then the Queen made me her Jubilee cat
I was given a medal and a silk feather hat.

What, she made you her Jubilee cat?
Did you ride in her carriage?

Yes, on my own velvet mat.

There is just one problem!
Yes, what's that?

Don't you know she has corgis …?

*Eden Latham, aged 10, is a pupil at St John's Walham Green
Church of England Primary School, Fulham, London SW6.*

Boogie in the Garden

Alexander Pirrie

*Buckingham Palace announced that a free pop
concert was to be held in the gardens of Buckingham
Palace to celebrate the Golden Jubilee.*

Hey there Queen!
Gonna boogie in the garden.
Boogie so loud
Gonna need a Royal Pardon.
Hip hop bash,
The roof will be raisin'.
You'll be tryin' not to hear us
Through the royal double-glazin'.
Not your scene?
You'll just have to lump it,
You can't always boogie
To the same royal trumpet.

Golden Jubilee, a right royal bash:
You can boogie in your garter,
You can boogie in your sash,
You can boogie with a sceptre,
You can boogie in a crown,
Man, they're gonna hear us
From the other end of town.

This party's out to prove
You're the best there's ever been,
As a hip hop happening
Cool mean QUEEN!

*Alexander Pirrie, aged 13, is a pupil at Edgehill College,
Bideford, Devon.*

Gold

Thomas Trevor-Roberts

Fifty golden wheat heads blow,
Fifty golden wheat stalks grow,
Golden years lay row on row,
Fifty years may quickly go.

Golden hair will quickly grey,
Golden wheat heads brown and fray,
Golden leaves will rot away,
Virtues are here to stay.

Thomas Trevor-Roberts, aged 12, is a pupil at Trevor-Roberts'
Preparatory School, London NW3.

Hairdresser Conversation

Claire Pelly

'How would you like your hair today
Blue rinses, highlights or curls?'
'Something pretty, something cool
Something to go with my pearls!'

'Is it a special occasion, Ma'am,
An event I might see on TV?'
'Nothing special, nothing grand
Just Tony Blair coming for tea!'

'So what are you doing this summer then,
I hear it's your grand Jubilee?'
'We're hoping to keep it a secret
Just my husband, the children and me.'

'Have you had your holidays yet,
Are you going any place far?'
'Just America, Spain and France
And I'm hoping to meet a Czar!'

'Are you doing any more shopping,
Or are you not staying in town?'
'I'm going to buy some dog food
And a Versace gown!'

Claire Pelly, aged 12, is a pupil at The Godolphin School,
Salisbury, Wiltshire.

Burmese, the Queen's Horse, speaks for the Cavalry

Laura Craigen

Now days grow short, nights more bleak
And our nostrils twitch with the scent of ice,
Boxed hay draws dust, and rain makes sleek
The cobbled yards. Winter broods beyond our sight,
Looming beneath the Cotswold knolls, and coldness bites.

I am Burmese. Aged now, rain-whipped flanks
To the wind, I wax grizzled and weathered,
Ice-flecked across my darkened shanks.
Winds lift my matted mane northwards: the first feathered
Flakes of winter tumble among the muddied heather.

It was not always desolate. Once, strong and raven-haired
From the woody halls I commanded plumed horses,
And my Queen, side-saddled and equally fair,
Rode upright and proud at the head of her forces.
But all grow older: age runs its course.

And now I bask wearily in windswept disuse.
With the seasons pass household equestrian faces,
And to the kettledrum's colourless, ancient tune
Colts grow, are broken, and are put through their paces –
Among bearskins and banners they seize time-honoured places.

As slow seasons turn, lost times are remembered,
Winter is dire but cannot sustain.
We are steel-shouldered with untapped labour:
Though the winter of technology seems to maintain
Its frosts, we huddle wordlessly, and do not complain.

For at Mons and at Cambrai they pushed bravely forward,
Our forefathers tussled at Bosworth, they claimed.
So we linger, we linger, and when winter is thawed
All the Queen's horses with all of her men
Shall hurtle in bright summer battle again.

*Laura Craigen, aged 18, is a pupil at
Wychwood School, Oxford.*

Ealasaid

Nina Matheson

Nad aonar, air a' chathair
Le clogad òir mud cheann
Gad dhìon bho na teangannan biorach a-muigh.

Cumaidh tu ort,
Le fiamh gàire, a' gabhail nam flùraichean,
Ag obair mar cheannard nad fhactaraidh.

An t-aodann ainmeil,
Eòlach, sìtheil, sàmhach
Na mo phòcaid gach latha gam chumail beò.

Tha na h-uile eòlach ort
Ach chan eil,
Tha thu fhèin eòlach, ach chan eil.

Chan eil e furasta,
A' cur ceann eòlach air pàiste,
Nad thaigh leis a' ghàrradh, stòlda, gun ghluasad,
    nad ghearastan.

A' coiseachd air an dùthaich, d'ealachan air loch,
Coin, eich, rèisean, cupa, teaghlach,
Eallaich is uallach Ealasaid.

*Nina Matheson, aged 17, is a pupil at Tain Royal Academy,
Ross-shire, Scotland.*

Elizabeth

Nina Matheson

Alone, on the throne,
With a golden helmet on your head
Defending you from the sharp tongues outside.

You carry on,
With a smile, accepting the flowers,
Working as head of your factory.

The famous face,
Familiar, peaceful, silent,
In my pocket each day keeping me alive.

Everyone knows you
But does not;
Connoisseur of the nodding acquaintance.

It is not easy,
Putting an experienced head on a youngster,
In your house with the garden, sedate, not moving,
    in your fort.

Walking in the country, your swans on a loch,
Dogs, horses, races, a cup, a family,
The burdens and responsibilities of Elizabeth.

The Queen's Hats

Helen Nightingale

A simple number, pretty nifty,
Was required in the nineteen-fifties.
In sixty-one I felt quite pensive;
My grey hat matched the comprehensives.
In sixty-six the grey was history;
I wore white for the World Cup victory.
In Vietnam, red showed my rage
For the napalmed girl on the world's front page.
As the seventies drew to a close
My fuchsia trilby stunned the discos.
But my lime green beret wasn't noticed at all
(eclipsed in eighty-nine by the Berlin Wall).
Communism fell, I was glad of that –
Capitalism means more hats.
My hat was black in Y-2-K;
I always knew that dome wouldn't pay.

I've always liked my hats. (At the moment I have pink.)
They give me an air of dignity, I think
Because a hat has more history than any crown jewel.
Though I know that as a ruler I'm not allowed much rule,
I've always had opinions – I've just hidden them with grace.
I'm more than just a hat stand and a pretty face.

*Helen Nightingale, aged 17, is a pupil at The Henley College,
Henley-on-Thames, Oxfordshire.*

A Recipe for the Golden Jubilee
(to Serve a Nation)

Take a carriage of full bodied tradition
add eight pints of blue blood, a pinch of gold dust
and a wave of white glove.

Breed two corgis, three thoroughbreds
sire with pomp and ceremony
and stir with an armed force.

Melt a seal of approval, mix in a pot of youth.
Stir in a season of debutantes with a golden ladle of grace.
Baste the rough beast of betrayal.

Clarify with some caring, whisk in a world of wisdom.
Grate in the pith of humour,
breaking the seal of secrets, and kneading an ink-stain of news.

Take a dollop of pride, beat in a beaver of guards.
Marinade the lineage for two score years and ten.
Let it prove for fifty years.

Bake blind on a red carpet.
Put in a palace and leave to ferment
in a jug of jubilee juice.

Place on the balcony to cool in the love and tears of a people.
Ride swans on the glaze of white icing,
sprinkle with tiaras and stars.

Add a topping of mercurial hats,
wrap with a ribbon of horses.
Portion to serve a nation.

*Key Stage 3 combined entry from James Brindley
Hospital School, Birmingham.*

Our Colours

Marta Ciechanowicz

Midsummer's day found me
Standing on
One of the Seven White Sisters.

I looked up
And saw a swallow,
And pondered.

It wore three colours;
Our colours.

Red, I thought,
The colour of the blush of shame
Of an Imperial past;
The smallest colour, but
Prominent; the colour of commoner's blood.

Blue dominates,
Cool blue of the British mind and
The Sea;
For Royal blood,
Our present.

And white, for
A peaceful future,
For freedom and democracy.

And the bird itself?
Small adventurer,
With the tenacious, wandering spirit of
Scott, Shackleton, MacArthur.

Drawing lines in the sky,
Yearly it unites
Past, now Commonwealth,
To present Kingdom, our Islands.

*Marta Ciechanowicz, aged 17, is a pupil at
St Catherine's School, Bramley, Surrey.*

What would a Queen have in her Pocket

Joseph Rogers

In her pocket she might have …

A large diamond,
A walky talky,
A bag of money,
A small leather purse,
How big is her pocket?

A lovely diamond ring,
A cup of coffee,
A golden walkman,
A bag of buttons,
How big is her pocket?

A jokebook,
A photograph,
A big brass key,
A lovely golden hairband,
How big is her pocket?

Joseph Rogers, aged 8, is a pupil at St Andrew's
Church of England School, Hove, Sussex.

Home Girl

Josephine Mbwana

*Dreams of an African girl growing up
in Elizabethan Britain*

Real.
I have never felt an elephant before,
But it was real.
I ran my hand across her side,
The long bristles scratched under my palm.
That was the highest I could reach.
My feet moved about on the lush, soggy grass,
Trying to stand on my tip-toes. This was no ordinary elephant.
The four extraordinarily tall tree trunks shuffled forward a little.
Was she nervous? Or was she trying to step on me?
I couldn't believe I was home again.
I could not believe I was in Africa.
Seriously. My house had gone.
So had the neighbours'. The mango tree remained;
And this strange, great, tender, beautiful beast
Stood before me instead.

I awoke. I was back inside my bed.
I looked out of the window, hoping for an African sun.
There was only English rain.
The woollen blanket was rolled up
Around me, over the duvet.
I closed my eyes and remembered. I ran my hand
Along the rolled-up bulk.
I was missing the sway, the scratching
Of the bristles. I was missing the most
Disgusting thing in the world.
A nose. The longest in the world.
I was missing my Africa.

*Josephine Mbwana, aged 17, is a pupil at St Margaret's School,
Bushey, Hertfordshire.*

[22]

The Queen's Golden Jubilee

Lucy Dunsford

Dawn breaking
Sun appearing
Day starting
England waking

Police forming
Crowds gathering
Pavements filling
Noise rising

Flags blowing
Colours blazing
Faces smiling
Excitement heightening

Horses sweating
Carriages rolling
Diamonds sparkling
Queen waving

Soldiers saluting
Cannons firing
People cheering
Bands playing

Country celebrating
Fifty years passing
Opinions changing
Monarchy continuing

Procession completing
Crowds dispersing
Noise subsiding
Rubbish appearing

Dusk approaching
Moon rising
Day ending
England sleeping

Lucy Dunsford, aged 14, is a pupil at St Helen's School,
Northwood, Middlesex.

Queen of the Dance

Brendan Davies

When old George died,
An era died with him.
A young girl, full of laughter; a princess at the dance
Took the yoke of responsibility
On her yet unburdened shoulders.

A husband to share her steps,
As she danced at honeymoon parties,
Blossomed as a mother,
Watched children grow in the palace garden
Dancing with daisychains.

In highland castles,
Warmed by Christmas hearths,
Corgis and faithful servants
Watch the whirling kilts to the skirl of the pipes
She smiles to welcome guests.

From faraway Queensland,
Proud Bushmen fly
To honour their 'Queen along England',
With drumming rhythms, painted feet beating dust
They dance for her and gloved fingers gently tap.

The coloured ranks in straight perfection
Troop by in arcs to the drum horse's beat,
Precise brass bands play the march,
Rows and rows of shiny feet convey
The salute to her most upright majesty.

In our homes on Christmas day
She brings stillness and calm to a turbulent world,
Meeting presidents and ministers
She is the anchor of many countries,
The Queen of the dance.

*Brendan Davies, aged 13, is a pupil at Pittville School,
Cheltenham, Gloucestershire.*

The Queen's Box

Leah Parker-Turnock

I will put in her box
the peace of the world turning around,
an album filled with joyful memories,
the smell of courage and faith.

I will put in her box
everlasting help to guide her on the way,
a sip of hot chocolate,
a glittering rare seal.

I will put in her box
the gift of talking to animals,
a last memory of a truthful friend,
a first helpful act of a new born child.

I will put in her box
a 13th season and a sunny world,
a real broomstick made out of fur,
a real horse made out of wood.

Her box is fashioned with
red velvet, silver bands,
with silver stars around the border,
and memories in the corner,
its hinges are like the opening of life.

She will sunbathe in her box
on the golden beach of Portsmouth,
then buy a scrumptious ice-cream,
and eat it by the dazzling seashore,
the colour of the hot golden sun.

Leah Parker-Turnock, aged 7, is a pupil at St Thomas of Canterbury Junior School, Chester.

Wanted: One Queen

Rachel Ponsford

Must be good at shaking hands,
Must know all the English lands.

A good person to make conversation,
Could enjoy a good vacation!

Must like corgis and horses,
Must have completed all manner of courses!

Willing to wear gloves and hats,
Must have a level six in SATs!

Able to say words 'My Husband and I',
And never, ever tell a lie.

Shiny teeth, not a tint of yellow in sight,
Must not start an argument or fight.

Never a hair out of place,
Must always pull a happy face.

A Queen should be pleasant and fair,
The most important thing the Queen does is to care.

*Rachel Ponsford, aged 11, is a pupil at Launceston
Community Primary School, Cornwall.*

Mrs Allagh-Wood

Jenny Wall

Mrs Allagh-Wood sits each day
Fingernails butterscotch yellow
Her heart glows fiercely,
Fizzing with pride
Jaded childless eyes
Have cried.

Mrs Allagh-Wood and her haphazard
Frames. Portholes of brass
Then chintz, plastic, now MDF.
Can such splintering bombs,
Such sparkling waltzing,
A rocket plunged up, up away
Really be held
And held just so
Englazed and untouchable
Behind the sugar glass?

Mrs Allagh-Wood's heart revels and swells.
Like daisy chains, she considers
The links from youth to here
Dipped in honey-sunshine
Or lucidly jaundiced and raw
Delighted shrieks of schoolgirl
To terrible shrieks of war.

Mrs Allagh-Wood considers, happy
She looks, she feels much more,
And her eyes remain upon that golden frame
Holding central
Our Gracious Queen.

Jenny Wall, aged 17, is a pupil at
The Belvedere School, Liverpool.

The Lady on My Bus Fare

Michael Binnie

The lady on my bus fare
Has reigned for 50 years
And in that time she's had her share
Of happiness and tears.
What thoughts run through the head that wears
The heavy, wobbly crown?
Is she sailing on Britannia still
Or going shopping down in town?
Is she dining with prime ministers
And delighting heads of state
Or giggling with Prince Philip
While washing dirty plates?
Do her hands turn purple
After all the folk she meets
Or does she fall asleep while watching
Coronation Street?
Speaking of Coronations,
Did she know back then
That her face would be imprinted
On coins and hearts of men?
My bus fare drips with raindrops
As I feed it into the slot.
The bus driver cops me a wink and says
'Hi kid, thanks a lot!'
The bus drives off quite smoothly
Without a hint of fuss
And Her Majesty comes to school with me …
Riding on my bus!

*Michael Binnie, aged 11, is a pupil at St Ninian's
Primary School, Dundee, Scotland.*

The Queen's Dolls' House

Megan Carson

Sitting there staring at it,
Longing to play with it,
Imagining yourself hoovering the little carpets.
'Dinnae scutch[1] 't,' says your nanny.
'Hut's[2] bruckle,[3] hut[4] isnae a wheeriorum.'[5]

Lying in bed dreaming of its little rooms.
Its cold and running water.
Then hearing your nanny's voice.
'Dinnae scutch 't, dinnae scutch 't!'
You wake up, it was a nightmare.

You're still not allowed to touch it.
It's stored in Windsor Castle.
It's been the story of your life.
Your best dolls' house.

1. touch
2. it's
3. fragile
4. it
5. toy

Megan Carson, aged 11, is a pupil at Holywood
Primary School, Dumfries-shire, Scotland.

The Wife, the Bairns and Me

Christine Paterson

Et wos 2nd o' June 1953
we were sat around the tely
The wife, the bairns and me
We had bin waitin' so long fer this dey
and, weth no delay,
we wotched The Queen's coranation day
The wife, the bairns and me

The keds kept wondering
'How can she keep a straight face?'
Ah wondered me self but thought
et wos jest te be nice
The croon jewels had us all enticed
The wife, the bairns and me
We wotched the croon be put on her heed
I knew smiles wood have the leed that nite
We cheered fer oor new Queen
Princess has been
The wife, the bairns and me

We herd knocking on oor door
people shooting and waving flags
the wains ran oot te join there wee friends
And we all celebrated on the street
The wife, the bairns and me

Christine Paterson, aged 11, is a pupil at Belmont Middle School,
Harrow Weald, Middlesex.

The Not-so-ordinary Day of Mrs Windsor

Tessa Riley

It felt like just an ordinary day.

The mail lay waiting on the mat,
the kettle whistled urgently.
The bacon sizzled sizzlingly,
and the toaster popped.

'Good morning.
This is the 8 o'clock News
on BBC Radio 4.
It is Tuesday, 4 June, 2002.
We lead today with the
    nationwide celebrations
for the Golden Jubilee
of Her Majesty,
Queen Elizabeth the Second.'

Perhaps it wasn't such an ordinary
    day after all.

Back in her bedroom
she folded her nightie
and patted her hair into place.
A dab of *Parfum de Paris* –
Ed's favourite scent –
and she was ready for the day.

The morning went before she knew.
Housekeeping over, left a glorious hour,
To potter,
alone,
sowing seeds in her greenhouse.

It's almost two.
Time to depart.
A celebratory sherry
and a Cup-a-Soup
(asparagus).

The last minute check:
• handbag
• tissues
• lipstick
    and …
• … tiara

Mrs Windsor
steps out to the uproar
and waves to her public
with pride and affection.

Not such an ordinary day after all.

*Tessa Riley, aged 17, is a pupil at Notting Hill and Ealing High School,
Ealing, London W13.*

Royal Mail

Megan Baddeley

I am the Queen.
No need of a camera, undeveloped negatives
Gathering dust.
Shelves empty of countless photo albums
Their use removed.
I see my printed face every morning
Letters at the breakfast table.
A face so well known
My country's name becomes irrelevant
A blank.
I've crept into other post codes too;
Nervously smiling, glacially patriotic.
My life's every importance recorded,
On show.
When I'm gone, my life's story will all be here –
The Post Office provides for every occasion.
I await the commemoration of my passing
And every day
My image is distorted thousands of times over
By unknown hands, showing
I've been paid for.

Megan Baddeley, aged 15, is a pupil at
St Edward's School, Oxford.

I Will Remember It Well

Helena Conroy-Lewis

Grandma remembers the Coronation,
After all, she had a day off work!
It was a colourful, glittery affair,
Music and splendour everywhere.
She watched it on a nine-inch TV.

And even though some rationing was still about,
Wonderful street parties were had throughout.
Clapping and cheering exploded
As it was learned that Everest was conquered.
Nevertheless, no matter the excitements that enthralled,
Grandad slept through it all.

Mum remembers the Silver Jubilee year:
She was studying for her 'O' levels (Oh dear!),
Virginia Wade won Wimbledon,
And Red Rum the National for the third time.
Nevertheless, no matter the excitements that enthralled,
Grandad slept through it all.

I will remember the Golden Jubilee.
Never mind the weather,
Or what world events occur,
There is one thing that's to be sure,
No matter the excitements that enthral,
Grandad will sleep through it all!

Helena Conroy-Lewis, aged 10, is a pupil at
La Retraite Swan, Salisbury, Wiltshire.

Two Little Girls

Alex Wicks

I saw a picture in a book,
And asked my gran to have a look.
'Two little girls, a lady and a mister,
Who are these girls?'
'That's the queen and her sister.
The two grown-ups are their mum and dad,
But that's years ago, lad.
Turn the page, you'll see a lady being crowned,
That's the little girl all grown up now.
On the next page this queen's got children of her own.

'Blimey,' said gran, 'how time's flown,
Now she's been queen for 50 years.'
A busy queen with no time for tears,
But I wonder if she ever has time to look
At a picture of two little girls in a book.

Alex Wicks, aged 10, is a pupil at Highfield
Primary School, Moortown, Leeds.

When They Were Alive

Anisa Bocus

They lie still in the museum
Just a display.
Lugers, Mausers, Machine Guns, Stick Grenades,
Land Mines, Doodlebug Bombs, Vintage Rifles,
All laid there to rest from the War.
When they were alive.
When they were alive, they roared with explosive rage,
Spitting bullets of hatred, often hitting home,
Spilling blood.
Scarlet rivers, mingled with rain and mud
And bodies of dead and dying men.
Screams and shouts of orders,
But the men closed their eyes,
Forever.
Now they lay, as though to rest,
Like hundreds of men in the graveyard –
Their tombs a permanent reminder
Of the bloodshed
And loss of lives of patriots,
Of the cost of War.
They lay there now, their days at an end too,
But always a threat,
As to what they still can do.

*Anisa Bocus, aged 15, is a pupil at Hackney Free and
Parochial Secondary School, London E9.*

Flamingo Football

Emily Mercer

Dreamed
I met the Queen
Alice-in-Wonderland style
raining hearts and roses
On a croquet flamingo

Someone
kicked a football
(or rolled up guinea-pig)
the winning goal
1966
And the crowd detonates

Now
she stands on the shore
waving to the dying sun
A champagne jubilee
And burning gold

*Emily Mercer, aged 12, is a pupil at Maharishi School,
Latham, Ormskirk, Lancashire.*

Inside the Queen's Suitcase

Kabir Sabir

Inside the Queen's suitcase is the heart of England.
Inside the heart of England lies the Queen's throne.
Inside the Queen's throne lies her caring.
Inside her caring lie all her charities.
Inside her charities are all the flowers.
Inside her flowers is all the happiness.
Inside her happiness is all the royal family.
Inside the royal family is all the wealth.
Inside the wealth is the Queen's suitcase.

Kabir Sabir, aged 9, is a pupil at Ercall Junior School,
Wellington, Shropshire.

The Secret Life of the Queen

Victoria Batten

Every night the queen wakes up,
When everyone else is asleep.
She climbs out of her four-poster bed.
And down the stairs she creeps.

She opens the door of Buckingham Palace,
And slips out into the night.
It's a good job no-one sees her in her Corgi pyjamas,
Because she would give them a fright.

Round the back of the palace,
There waits the queen's motorbike,
But before roaring it into life,
She checks if there's anyone in sight. (There isn't.)

So she switches on her motorbike,
But it does not make a sound.
Instead it leaps high into the air,
And about six foot off the ground.

She decides to see her friend called Ben,
Who works on the underground.
He drives the trains round late at night,
When no-body else is around.

When she finally finds her friend called Ben,
With him she has a cup of tea.
But flies off back to the palace,
Before dawn has come to be.

So if you're in London late at night,
You may see the queen in the sky.
Riding her magic motorbike,
On which she likes to fly.

*Victoria Batten, aged 11, is a pupil at Lady Joanna
Thornhill Primary School, Ashford, Kent.*

Garvaghy Road

Naomi Miller

The path is lined with a wall of shields.
Numbly we walk down, hating, hating.
Hating the people screaming at us,
Shouting names, throwing stones.
One man yelled he'd kill us soon.
We believed him and froze,
Savouring our life while we had it.
But he was wrestled back by a policeman
Armed and ready with his tear gas and rubber bullets,
Whilst we walked down that 50-metre, mile-long road.
Some of us cried, but I set my teeth fast,
Squeezed my knees together to stop them shaking.
The world had moved on, but wars stayed the same.
We had the Beatles and fighting, the Spice Girls and fighting,
Everything and nothing have changed.
But I preferred before, when it was innocent.
We're almost at the end of the walk –
From insecurity to safety
Just a few steps now, clinging to each other's hands.
Just because we're different.
The daily walk to school.

*Naomi Miller, aged 12, is a pupil at
Oxford High School, Oxford.*

My Crown Jewels

Megan Rotherham

My Sceptre would be made,
Of chocolate and ice cream,
Jelly laces winding down,
And dotted with fluffy cream.

Then my Orb would be a ball,
Of string covered in glue,
Dipped in glitter, painted gold,
And I would stick a paper cross,
On the top to finish off.

Now my Crown would be made,
Of willow branches,
Of little leaves and flying bugs,
But to finish it off, sprinkled with dew,
To make it sparkle in the sun.

The Sword would be made,
Of blue ink and paint,
Sprinkled with stars,
And dipped in the moon,
Fought with by knights,
And kept in the Tower.

That is how I would like,
My Crown Jewels to be made,
When I am Queen.

*Megan Rotherham, aged 9, is a pupil at Sutton Valence
Preparatory School, Chart Sutton, Kent.*

On Guard

Ellen Proudfoot

Boots as black as coal,
So shiny you see your face in them,
Long stiff black trousers,
Cosy rosy red coat, brass buttoned right to the top,
A huge hat, like a whole family of hedgehogs sitting
On his head.
His face as straight as his back.
He doesn't blink at cameras,
Laugh at jokes,
Or make polite conversation.
He's not being stuffy or mean,
His job is to guard the Queen.

Ellen Proudfoot, aged 10, is a pupil at St Katharine's School,
St Andrews, Scotland.

Elizabeth's Cousin

Martin Dubois

There is a melancholic old tramp who sits on a dirty step
Holding out a paper cup to the bored workers bustling by.
His toes peep out of his shoes, and he keeps a wispy, tangled beard.
I sometimes sit with him, quietly staring up at St Paul's
He has forgotten how to smile but wistfully thumbs the same ten-pence piece.

He once wrestled with words, spoke to me in hoarse, shred-like breaths.
'D'you know … she doesn't get any older – does she?'
Looking at the coin with sunken eyes, and then returning to my gaze.
'No, no … I suppose she doesn't,' but was violently tugged towards snatching it
And dashing towards the river with sole, destructive intent.

Crumpled within his messy pockets are some commemorative stamps
Which emerge on sunny days, and pass the piteous hours of beggary.
'D'you know,' cough-cough-splutter, 'you could use this as a bus fare?'
Blurting out a few, regal words each time we sit, watching time drift
Has built up a mutual distrust. He no longer seems Dickensian.

Going to the procession, and empowered by some soup and bread
His eyes are lighter – brown not black – and he speaks with softer vowels.
'She's my cousin, you know,' smugly eyeing my reaction with awkward smile.
Is there some truth in this? His slim nose ridges similarly
But the grime that dusks his face makes it impossible to tell.

Bundling to the front, buoyed by his revelations, he seems oddly imperial
And cries 'Happy Jubilee, cousin Elizabeth!' with all his might.
People look at him: eccentric, sentimental old fool with a funny smell.
But it is my sentimentality, watching his intimate preservation of majestic glance
And entertaining ideas of royal affinity, which makes me want to believe.

Martin Dubois, aged 17, is a pupil at
Wimbledon College, London SW19.

My Lady

Katy Vincent

Here I stand
With my friends at my side
Awaiting another day.

A skittish breeze
Sends the leaves
Chasing each other down the long drive.

The dawn breaks
And the hustle of morning
Starts again.

With gold trim
My vermillion saddle cloth
Is smoothed gently over my strong back.

With heavy gold bridle
The cold steel bit
Is slipped into my mouth.

'Crisp morning today, lad'
Is whispered in my ear.
As I step out in the cold dawn.

A shiver of excitement
And I stand proud and strong
As a lady of gold slips lightly into my saddle.

With ears alert
And nostrils wide
We walk together through the throng.

Hordes of people
Waving flags, raising cheers
My lady guides me through the crowds
A Sun amongst her stars.

*Katy Vincent, aged 10, is a pupil at
Kingsbury Hill House School, Marlborough, Wiltshire.*

Untitled

Luke Bennison

*Prompted by watching the Air Ambulance
from the schoolroom window.*

I heard a noise.
It was getting louder.
I saw a red helicopter.
Big and shiny with enormous propeller blades.
Lying in a vast, green field, it was surrounded by fences, trees, cars
    and police officers.
By the helicopter was a red carpet and the door opened slowly
    and out came the queen.
She waved to everyone.
She tiptoed out.
She was wearing a glamorous dress with gloves and a hat to match.
She walked down the red carpet elegantly and walked to
    a little room.
The shiny helicopter's propellers started to turn and the helicopter
    took off like the speed of light.

*Luke Bennison, aged 13, is a pupil at Plymouth Hospital
School, Plymouth, Devon.*

The Queen

Emily Colley

In the yard
There is
A palace

In the palace
There is
A room

In the room
There is
A throne

On the throne
There is
A queen

On the queen
There is
A crown

*Emily Colley, aged 9, is a pupil at Great Bentley
Primary School, Colchester, Essex.*

Jubilee Pizza

Katie Leafe

To prepare your Jubilee Pizza
you will need to find
ingredients from all over the world.

To create the great, golden crust
you will need to chop finely
the bold colours of the Union Jack
and stir vigorously,
then add five sparkling diamonds
from your royal crown.
Spread the mixture out
and place it in the oven.
After approximately five minutes
you will hear the cheering
of many people preparing to meet you.

Sprinkle gifts, that you have received
from different countries around the world,
over the golden crust
and arrange fifty silver carriages
around the edge.
Chop up a couple of notes
from the famous National Anthem
and place them in the centre.

Serve all this on a bed made
from the Scottish, English, Australian
and New Zealand flags.
Then enjoy your fifty years of ruling England.

*Katie Leafe, aged 13, is a pupil at Thornden School,
Chandler's Ford, Hampshire.*

Media Molehills

Emma Ballantine Dykes

I know the routine.
Flanked on all sides
By wilting flowers and eyeless smiles,
Burning cameras target my face,
Dark weapon-like machines
That swallow me whole and sear my shadow onto paper.

Uncertain.
I wear my painted face with conviction.
Yet even as I smile and wave
I know the headlines are being written,
And endless suited editors are sipping lattes
And cutting me down to size.

I will discover tomorrow
what the world thinks I should have said and done.
Whatever I do, either way, is analysed in columns,
Given a mark out of ten,
Compared with the last time,
Compared with someone who did it better.

But I have learnt
that a new paper will be printed tomorrow,
The flowers will fade in their vase,
and fifty years from now
The way I shook their hands and smiled,
Will be as crucial as a pixel in a beautiful picture.

*Emma Ballantine Dykes, aged 15, is a pupil at
The Godolphin School, Salisbury, Wiltshire.*

The Crown Jewels

Sarah Grant

Sparkling diamonds with facets of fire,
Glinting and glittering when caught by the sun,
Cold flinty onyx stones like granite cliffs,
Worn smooth by the endless battles with the restless tides.

Blushing red rubies like young floating brides,
Leaving the safety of their nests for the first time,
Envy green emeralds with their sly winking edges,
And their faultlessly cut sides; outwardly innocent.

Cool hard topaz stones deep in thought,
Reflecting the swirling, heaving, frothing oceans,
The shining opals; flashing the colours of the rainbow,
Encased in heavy rails of gold.

Soft baby pearls, hung on a chain,
Glowing with a mystic eerie light,
Harsh yellow amber – a contrast to the pearls,
Opaque and thickly mixed like a pot of creamy paint.

Fiery amethysts with their dangerous message,
Showing different moods and faces at each shimmer,
The carnelian with its blood red reminders,
Of the battles long since faded from the fickle English mind.

And with all their different messages and appearances,
All gems combine to serve Her Majesty,
Like her loyal subjects, all different, but all eager,
To pay homage to The Throne in its regal splendour.

*Sarah Grant, aged 15, is a pupil at the London Jewish
Girls High School, Hendon, London NW4.*

The Game of Truth

Michael Hart

In the sunlit garden,
Where the tall trees grew,
Two little noble girls
Sat amongst the dew.

'Let's play a game!'
Elizabeth said,
'I'll be the Queen
With a crown upon my head.'

'I'll be the princess,'
Margaret cried.
'I'll wear a lovely dress
With a prince at my side.'

Their mother and father
Watched from the door,
As the two girls danced
On a ballroom floor.

After an hour,
They were making speeches,
And then at the feast
They were eating fresh peaches.

They were really having
So much fun,
But at the end of the day,
Their game was done.

Was it a coincidence?
Nobody knew,
But their little game
Was about to come true.

Michael Hart, aged 14, is a pupil at Pope Pius X Catholic
High School, Wath, South Yorkshire.

Bàrdachd na Bàn-rìgh

Naomi Cherry

Tro chruadal is glòir bidh i gar stiùireadh
Bidh i cuideachadh càch gu coibhneil
Airson cuideachadh a thoirt ann an dòigh air choreigin
A beatha ar dùthaich, ar dùthaich a beatha.

Bidh ar dùthaich a' cur earbsa innte
Agus cha dìobair i iad
Bidh ar dùthaich a'creidsinn innte
A beatha ar dùthaich, ar dùthaich a beatha.

Chan e draoidh a th'innte
Ach tha coltas oirre
Olc air a cheannsachadh, mathas a' tilleadh
A beatha ar dùthaich, ar dùthaich a beatha.

Bidh i a' tagradh na h-uile bhuaipe fhèin
Agus bho a teaghlach cuideachd
Bidh i dìcheallach ann an gliocas
A beatha ar dùthaich, ar dùthaich a beatha.

Naomi Cherry, aged 13, is a pupil at Glenalmond College, Perth, Scotland.

The Poem for the Queen

Naomi Cherry

Through hardship and glory she leads us well
The help she gives others of a generous nature
Wishing to help in some way
Her life our country, our country her life.

Our country puts its trust in her
And she will not forsake them
Our country believes in her
Her life our country, our country her life.

She is no magician
But she seems to be
Evil is conquered, goodness is retrieved
Her life our country, our country her life.

She demands all of herself
And of her family also
She is steadfast in wisdom
Her life our country, our country her life.

Through my Eyes

Kate Hamilton

Some people may think
I see public appearances
as a chore,
a necessary task – but
they do not see things
from my view.
They have not felt
the excitement running through me
as I see
people lining the streets, hoping
for a glimpse of me:
their Queen.
They cannot imagine
how it feels
to be greeted
with waving flags,
and cheering voices.
To be presented with flowers,
wherever I go.
Shouts of 'Your Majesty',
Words I could never tire of.
They do not understand that
every handshake is a thrill.
Each bouquet
A welcome gift.
Every flag raised,
a great honour.
And every poem written,
a verse of pride.

Kate Hamilton, aged 15, is a pupil at King's School,
Macclesfield, Derbyshire.

Black African

Patsy Amadi

Coffee coloured skin
Big broad nose
An embroidered head tie
Tames my wild afro
Brightly coloured garments
Hug my rounded hips
Ravishing red 'rouge à levre'
On my full lips
Bold brown eyes
Watch in admiration
The image on the glass
Groomed to perfection
Heirlooms, precious jewels
Residues of my ancestry
Black British? Black other?
Black African Queen.

Patsy Amadi, aged 17, is a pupil at St Michael's Catholic Grammar School, Finchley, London N12.

To Become a Queen

Lydia Wilding-Smith

To become a Queen you need:
A royal marinade from birth,
A silver spoon of politeness.
Fold in honour to your country,
Finally add some ground confidence.
Now sip tea.
Wait,
Allow ingredients to blend for 50 years.
Once cooked this is the definitive recipe for an English Queen.

Lydia Wilding-Smith, aged 12, is a pupil at
Newnham Middle School, Bedford.

The Fire at Windsor

Sinead Costelloe

A tiny, tiny prick of flame,
Emerges in the palace.
It softly grows, it slowly spreads,
An angry yellow malice.

It rips and tears, destroys and kills,
The beauty of the palace.
It has a goal; to eat and take
The rugs, the jewels, the chalice.

It wants to take, it means to rape
The great heart of the palace.
The wasps lash out their fiery sting.
It's warm; it's vile; it's callous.

But though the fire may swarm and rage
In the great depths of the palace,
Windsor will turn another page,
Defeat the bitter furnace.

*Sinead Costelloe, aged 12, is a pupil at Queen Anne's School,
Caversham, Berkshire.*

Untitled

Genevieve Raghu

I bought a scarf, a barricade
For February's bitter blows.
Its bully wind and the battering
My being now fully knows.

I was buying my scarf, fringed and black
When the assistant, gossipy, said:
'Did you hear the news? This morning?
Did you know Margaret is dead?'

Two lives, two worlds remote
Though in one island we are rooted
Yet in passing, your neat pastels I admired
And those practised waves justly noted.

But now, with this news
I wondered if we might at least share
The numbness, perhaps, that comes
With loss, when emotions are laid bare.

A father and now, a sister gone
You grieve, and I, my own special king
For a moment in time we melt and blend
Whirled like a top by the February wind.

There's a strange conflict ahead
With the celebration of your reign
For in a shadow
Memories of loss remain.

*Genevieve Raghu, aged 14, is a pupil at
Norwich High School for Girls, Norfolk.*

The Veggie National Anthem

Stella McCall

Sun shine on our growing green
Don't wilt our growing green
Sun save the green
Send her asparagus
Lettuce and cauliflower
(And lots of sunflower)
Please rain over her
Sun save the green.

*Stella McCall, aged 10, is a pupil at Kinloch Primary School,
Carnoustie, Angus, Scotland.*

The Queen

Connor Trendell

A solid figure in a blurry world
Never changing nor moving
Speaking little and doing lots
A seeming tortoise surrounded by hares.

She shows little emotion
Never confrontational, never controversial
Told what to say by helpers and aides
Never speaking freely or saying her mind.

Never working in a lifetime
Seeming to live off other people's efforts
Unable to live normally or freely
Trapped in a title, a name.

The real Queen will never be known,
Her personality, beliefs and feelings,
Hidden by a perfect image,
Behind a shroud of mystery.

Stuck in an image created by others
Never free to speak or do,
To never be herself
To act the perfect person
Detached from me or you.

The real Queen must have determination
To get through the things she has to do.
To never be herself
Or get angry
To be like ice in a burning fire.

A steady figure in a turbulent world,
Kind to all and nasty to none.
Never angry nor mean
A solid rock in a beach of sand.

Developing over time
Blossoming into stately ruler
Ever changing with the developing world,
A chameleon fitting to every background.

Ruling through turbulent times
Never wavering, standing firm,
Reacting to all events with dignity
Constantly self controlled and faithful.

*Connor Trendell, aged 14, is a pupil at George Heriot's School,
Edinburgh, Scotland.*